Summer 2009

To the Payne Family,

Knut-Eric Joslin

Summer 2009

To the Payne Family,

OSLO

THE VIKING CAPITAL

Oslo, the capital of Norway, is situated between the Oslo Fjord and the large expanses of forest surrounding its periphery. It is an ancient city, with a history predating the Viking Age.

Oslo has expanded down through the ages from being a large little town to becoming a moderately small, modern metropolis. Despite this, it has managed to retain an intimate and relaxed atmosphere.

Oslo has everything! Historical architecture, large parks and small, the sea as well as small forest lakes, first class restaurants and small cozy cafés. And best of all: many of the sights Oslo has to offer are within walking distance of the center of town and the main avenue, Karl Johan.

Oslo offers all kinds of entertainment. And it is a city for all seasons: spring is short and hectic, summer bright and warm, fall is the season for great cultural events and during winter, cross-country skiing and all of the other winter sports are avidly pursued. For as everyone knows, Norwegians are born with skis on their feet!

Today Oslo is a modern city, but it is also a city with deep roots in the past. It is just this blend of the new and the old that makes Oslo one of Europe's most charming cities.

visit OSLO

Oslo Visitors and Conventions Bureau

CONTENTS

N·W·DAMM&SØN

OSLO'S HISTORY

Oslo appeared as a small village 1000 years ago in Gamlebyen, at the foot of Ekeberg, where the Alna River ran out into the Oslo Fjord. We know very little about this period of the city's history, because the settlement was built of small wooden houses that were clustered so closely together, that whole sections of the settlement burnt down during a fire. It wasn't until the 12th century that a number of buildings were built in stone.

We have many ruins from this period, the majority of which are situated in the area called *Middelalder-byen* (Medieval Oslo) that has recently been developed. Here we can view the ruins of St.Clement's Church from the 12th century, the Church of St. Mary from the same period, and St.Hallvard's, Oslo's first cathedral, which was built during the 12th century, and in use until the 1660s. The remains of the old Bishop's Castle can be seen below Oslo Ladegård (Oslo Manor House). The name Ladegård stems from its original function of supplying Akershus Fortress with food. The building that stands today was erected in 1720. The Baroque Room inside is used for concerts, and the beautifully landscaped surroundings were modeled after a Baroque garden.

After the fire of 1624 that destroyed old Oslo, King Christian IV decided that the new city should be built under the shelter of Akershus Fortress. The new city was named after him and called Christiania, a name that it retained until 1925, at which time it was again called Oslo.

"The city shall lie here", said King Christian IV. His wish was granted and the city was named after him as well.

The Old Manor House has a beautiful Baroque garden.

THE SHIPPING CITY

The Oslo Fjord cuts into Norway's southern landmass from Skagerrak to Oslo. The Fjord is 100 kilometers long, and is an open, hospitable fjord with many beautiful islands and thousands of skerries and reefs.

At the end of the fjord is Oslo, an important seaport and the capital of the country. The city has a busy harbor with daily ferry connections to Fredrikshavn, Hirtshals and Copenhagen in Denmark, to Helsingborg in Sweden, and to Kiel in Germany.

During the summer, cruise ships from around the world dock in the harbor beneath the ancient Akershus Fortress. In front of City Hall, fishing boats sell the night's catch, and private boats hurry back and forth. The harbor is full activity during the short and hectic summer months.

The Fjord is also an important recreation arena, teeming with bathers and boats the whole summer long. And when the fjord freezes over during the winter, you can see many ice-fishing enthusiasts waiting patiently for their catch.

The inner Oslo Fjord has its own little archipelago. Hovedøya is the island that lies closest to the city's center. It doesn't take more than 10 minutes by ferry to get there. On the island are the Ruins of a Cistercian monastery founded by English monks in the year 1147, but destroyed by a fire in 1532. The Ruins make their presence felt in the landscape so this is a place one visits out of respect. Hovedøya has a totally unique and protected plant life with many rare flowers thanks not least to the monks of the monastery.

Oslo City Hall

Hvervenbukta

Hovedøya Abbey Ruins

DOWNTOWN OSLO

Considering that Oslo is a city with approximately 500,000 inhabitants, it is surprisingly small. In fact it is one of the smallest capitals in the world. It is also an open and hospitable city. The city's main boulevard, Karl Johans gate, is named after one of Norway's kings, who was a general under Napoleon. The avenue extends from Oslo's Sentralstasjon (main train station) as far as the Royal Castle.

Many of the city's main attractions are situated within walking distance from this street. This is where you will find the theatres, Stortinget (Parliament), the most famous shops and exclusive hotels.

Oslo Rådhus (Oslo City Hall), inaugurated in 1950 and the pride of the city, is the seat of the city's political and administrative leadership. Oslo Rådhus is also the focus of international attention when the Nobel Peace Prize is awarded on December 10th each year.

The Royal Castle sits majestically at the top of Slottsparken (the Royal Gardens). The Castle was built as the main residence for King Carl Johan. It was designed by the famous architect Hans Ditlev Franciscus Linstow, and was completed in 1849. Today the castle is the private residence of King Harald V and Queen Sonja, while the Crown Prince Couple Haakon Magnus and Mette Marit reside at the family's Skaugum Estate in Asker on the outskirts of Oslo.

The Parliament Building

The National Theatre

The small green park called Spiker-suppa (lit. "nail soup") lies between Stortinget and Nationaltheatret (the National Theatre). During the summer it boasts a fountain and wading pool; in winter, the city's small but busy central skating rink called Narvisen.

The Nobel Peace Center opened in 2005. The center presents all winners and their work, Alfred Nobel and the Prizes and is open to the public every day.

In compliance with Alfred Nobel's testament, the Norwegian Nobel Committee awards one of the most prestigious prizes in the world, the Nobel Peace Prize, to a worthy candidate each year on December 10th. The award ceremony takes place in Oslo City Hall, with members of the Norwegian Royal Family and a number of Norwegian and international celebrities present.

Oslo Domkirke (Oslo Cathedral) faces Stortorget, and was inaugurated in 1697. It was originally a rather modest church – there was simply not enough money to build anything more imposing. But after being remodeled a number of times, the cathedral has become worthy of the city of Oslo. It was in this church the Crown Prince and his bride were married in 2001.

The Norwegian artist Dagfin Wærenskiold designed the large bronze doors dominating the facade and the stained glass windows in the church were created by Emanuel Vigeland, the brother of Gustav Vigeland, the artist behind the sculptures in Vigelandsparken.

The 17th of May, Norway's Constitution Day, is an important event. Thousands of rejoicing schoolchildren parade up Karl Johans gate, past the Storting until they reach the Royal Palace, where they are greeted by the royal family from Slottsbalkongen (the castle's public balcony).

Town planning during the 60's and 70's had a number of unfortunate consequences for the city. Among other things, the city was cut off from the harbor when the streets were widened to accommodate increased traffic. By channeling all through traffic through a tunnel, however, the problem has now been corrected and Oslo appears once again as the seaport that it is. Recent traffic planning has also made Oslo a better-organized city, and accessibility has improved considerably.

Oslo Sentralstasjon is the city's train station. It connects the country's eastern and western railway networks, with tracks running through the Oslo Tunnel.

Oslo's Gardermoen Airport is situated 50 kilometers from the city's center, and is the main airport for all domestic and international flights for the Oslo region.

THE MUSEUMS

Many of the city's museums are also located in the center of town. Nasjonalgalleriet's (the national art museum of Norway) collection includes works of art from all over the world as well as Norwegian art up to 1945. *The Sick Child* and *The Scream*, two of Edvard Munch's most famous paintings, as well as the most famous example of national romanticism, *Brudeferden i Hardanger* (The Wedding Party at Hardanger) by the painters Tiedemand and Gude, are hanging here.

Stenersensmuseet, with three important collections of Norwegian and international art, is one of the city's newest art museums. The museum also arranges temporary exhibitions.

Museet for Samtidskunst (the National Museum of Contemporary Art) is another museum worth visiting in Oslo. It's collection covers Norwegian art from 1945 onwards, and is housed in Norges Bank's imposing old building at Bank-plassen.

The privately owned Astrup Fearnley Museum of Modern Art, on the other hand, was built with the intention of being a museum, and has an impressive permanent collection of modern European and American art and has regular guest exhibitions as well.

Kunstnernes Hus is situated across from Slottsparken. It is here that Norway's most loved and hated exhibition, Høstutstillingen (the National Annual Autumn Exhibition), is arranged in September each year.

The National Museum of Contemporary Art

The Astrup Fearnley Museum of Modern Art

Nasjonalgalleriet (The national art museum of Norway)

The International Museum of Children's Art drawn by Anton Antonov, 13 years old, Russia.

A Doll's House by Henrik Ibsen is staged all over the world, and is the renowned playwrite's most famous play.

Henrik Ibsen made a daily visit to Grand Café on Karl Johans gate, where he always sat at the same table. It was said that he was so punctual that you could set your watch by him.

HENRIK IBSEN

No Norwegian author is more inter-nationally famous than Henrik Ibsen. The apartment where Henrik Ibsen lived the last years of his life, it too a stone's throw from the Palace, has now become a museum where guided tours, lectures and literary events are arranged. It was here, in this apartment in Drammensveien by the Palace, that Ibsen wrote *Johan Gabriel Borkman* and *When We Dead Awaken.*

AKERSHUS

Akershus Festning is a vital and imposing part of the harbor view. Construction of the Fortress began over 700 years ago, and was considered at the time to be one of the most secure fortresses in all of Scandinavia. Many attempts were made to besiege Akershus Festning over the years, but it always managed to repel the attacks. King Christian IV modernized the fortress during the 1590's and built a new castle, Akershus Castle, in the Renaissance style.

During WWII, the German invaders took control of the fortress. Forty-two Norwegian resistance fighters were executed here. A monument honoring these men is placed at the entrance of the Castle.

The Armed Forces Museum at Akershus Festning documents this difficult period in the history of the country.

Today the castle is used by the government for official dinners.

Aside from the section of the fortress that is occupied by the military, Akershus Festning is open to the public. A spectacular view of the harbor can be seen from the fortress rampart.

The steel sculpture "Marriage" by the American sculptor Tony Smith, was a gift from the American Carter-Menil Human Rights Foundation to the Norwegian people: "To the People of Norway for their contribution to peace". The sculpture was presented by ex-President Jimmy Carter.

Aker Brygge

Akershus Festning

AKER BRYGGE

While Akershus Festning has remained untouched for hundreds of years, Aker Brygge, on the other side of the harbor, has undergone enormous change.

After having completed its last construction at the end of the 1970's, an oil platform destined for the North Sea, the shipping yard Akers Mekaniske Verksted was closed down. The entire area of the shipyard was then submitted to a total facelift and has now become a modern city complex with luxury apartments, offices, theaters, movie theaters, shops and a large number of restaurants. A number of gifted architects have succeeded in combining the old factory halls with modern architecture.

During the summer months Aker Brygge is alive with activity. The crowds stroll, have a glass of beer at one of the many outdoor restaurants, or just sit on the edge of the pier with a bag of fresh shrimp. Summer in the city and Aker Brygge are inseparable.

Early in the morning, fishing boats pull up at the City Hall pier with the night's catch. They sell cod and pollack, but during the summer their freshly-steamed shrimp are most popular.

CHRISTIANIA TORG AND KVADRATUREN

Each of Oslo's neighborhoods has its unique charm. Kvadraturen, Oslo's historic inner city situated behind Akershus Festning, is a part of town that has been renovated in recent years. A major landmark here is Christiania Torv, the city's original marketplace, before Stortorget took over this function. There are many private galleries in this part of town, such as Fotogalleriet (Photographers' Gallery), Norske Grafikere (the Association of Norwegian Graphic Artists) and Norsk Form (Center for Design, Architecture and the Built Environment). There is an abundance of restaurants and cafés as well, such as the venerable Gamle Raadhus (the old City Hall), with the Theater Museum on the second floor, Engebret Café, or the more exclusive Statholdergaarden.

Engebret Café

Celcius Café

The Old City Hall Restaurant

LIVELY NIGHTLIFE

The people of Oslo enjoy going out and in recent years a myriad of new cafés, restaurants and bars have appeared and nightlife has flourished. The venerable Theatercafeen in Hotel Continental represents the old café tradition, while the French-inspired Pascal in Drammensveien can be said to represent the new. Pascal received worldwide attention when the President of the United States at the time, Bill Clinton, made an impromptu stop at the café during his official visit to Norway.

While Norwegian cuisine was relatively simple compared to the Continent just a few years ago, it is now of a very high standard. Young Norwegian chefs compete with colleagues all over the world, and restaurants like Bagatelle and Oro are included in the Michelin Diners' Guide.

Coffee bars that serve *cafe crème, cafe con leche* or an *espresso* — no one asks for just "coffee" any more — have sprouted all over the city.

The food revolution does not only apply to Norwegian cuisine; the city is also teeming with food from all over the world. You can eat Thai, Chinese, Moroccan, Greek, Italian, Mongolian, Lebanese, Egyptian, Indian, Japanese or American food — all in Oslo.

The Ekeberg Restaurant

Café Pascal

Theatercaféen

FROGNER PARK

Frogner Park is a popular recreation area for the city's inhabitants, in summer as in winter. It is Oslo's largest park, as well as being the city's greatest tourist attraction. It is internationally famous because it is one of the world's largest sculpture parks. All of the over 200 sculptures decorating the park were made by the sculptor Gustav Vigeland (1859-1943), who donated this entire collection to the city of Oslo under the condition that it provide the necessary grounds for mounting it. Vigeland's geometrical park design is baroque in its basic shape, but is also influenced by neoclassicism. Construction of the park began in 1930, but the large fountain was not completed until 1947, four years after Vigeland's death. The grounds contain 200 sculptures composed of over 650 figures.

Vigeland's monumental art is a source of enthusiasm as well as indignation. Most famous among the sculptures are the 17-meter-high *Monolith* in granite which is situated at the Park's highest point, and the little bronze sculpture *Sinnataggen*, *("Angry Boy")* which is mounted on the bridge of sculptures. One of the most monumental in format is the large fountain composed of a giant basin held up by six men.

There is a visitor's center with a café, information and a souvenir shop by the main entrance.

Oslo Bymuseum (the Oslo City Museum) is also located in Frogner Park. The museum allows you to follow the history of the capital in idyllic surroundings. The Park has several pleasant restaurants, and not far off is the Vigeland Museum, which is dedicated entirely to the artist Gustav Vigeland. And if you feel like swimming, you can visit the outdoor swimming pool, Frogner-badet, at the north end of the Park.

Frogner Park

Frogner Swimming Pool

Vestkanten (Oslo`s west end), with its many houses of architectural interest, is located between Frogner Park and the center of town. Bogstadveien, which extends from Majorstuen to downtown Oslo, is one of the city's most exclusive shopping areas.

Homansbyen, behind the Royal Palace, is one of the city's exclusive residential areas. Many of the facades of these houses, built during the 1890's, are richly ornamented.

Angry Boy

Vigeland Museum

The Silo at Grünerløkka is one of the city's most innovative buildings. Once the city's largest grain silo, it now houses the city's students.

GRÜNERLØKKA

Akerselva, the main river that divides the city in two, has its source in the large forest north of the city. It is possible to follow the river from its mouth in the Oslo Fjord all the way to its source at Maridalsvannet, the city's largest reservoir in Nordmarka.

Grünerløkka lies on the east side of the river and was until recent times a typical, rather worn, residential area for laborers with little of interest for a potential visitor. But in the course of the last twenty years, Grünerløkka has undergone an urban renewal process. Grünerløkka has become a popular residential area, especially among the younger generations.

Many of the city's most trendy restaurants and cafés are to be found here, and Grünerløkka is today an attractive neighborhood for those who live there, as well as for visitors.

Grünerløkka has become a popular residential area, especially for the younger generation, but a few old idyllic spots still remain...

Ole Enstad's sculpture "Divers" extends over Akerselven.

The Hotel Oslo Plaza and Galleri Oslo.

GRØNLAND

The name Grønland refers to green grass and open meadows. It is no longer the case in the neighborhood of Grønland, which has long since been fully developed. Great changes have occurred in this part of town as well. The most dilapidated buildings have been torn down and the neighborhood has undergone extensive renewal.

Grønland is in a state of flux. This part of town has become very popular among young people in search of housing, which in turn results in the appearance of new cafés and restaurants and a revitalization of the neighborhood. Grønland is also known for its many ethnic shops. This is where you go to purchase inexpensive fresh produce or exotic fruit.

The large mosque in Åkerbergveien, and the hotel Radisson SAS Plaza are two monumental new buildings located in this part of town.

EDVARD MUNCH AT TØYEN

Edvard Munch is Norway's most famous artist. He left his 1100 paintings, 15,500 graphic prints, 4700 drawings and six sculptures, together with printing plates, books, photographs and documents, to the City of Oslo. In this way more than half of the artist's work is owned by the city. The Munch Museum at Tøyen is a museum of international standard.

Adjacent to the Museum are the Geological and Zoological Museums as well the city's beautiful Botanical Gardens. From here it is a short walk to Oslo's largest public swimming pool, Tøyenbadet, which also boasts a large outdoor swimming pool during the summer.

The Munch Museum

Kampen

The traditional workers' district, Kampen, is within walking distance of Tøyen. It's advantageous location on the top of a hill as well as its many quaint wooden houses; make it a popular residential area.

Tøyen Swimming Pool

The Zoological Museum

The Botanical Garden

IDYLLIC SPOTS IN THE MIDDLE OF THE BIG CITY

It doesn't take more than a few minutes to walk from Karl Johan, up Akersgaten, to St. Olav's Church, the city's main Catholic church. Behind it lies a quiet, idyllic neighborhood full of old, restored wooden houses. Some are found in Akersbakken, but the majority are in Damstredet and Telthusbakken, a short distance away. The city's oldest church, Gamle Aker Kirke, is also located here. It is not only used for church services; it's excellent accoustics and medieval interior make it ideal for religious and medieval music concerts.

From the top of Telthusbakken is a panoramic view of the east side of the city. Dominating the view is the old grain silo by Akerselva, which was intended to be torn down but instead, has been turned into student residences.

For a pleasant walk, descend Telthusbakken to Akerselva and then follow the path along the river back to the center of town.

Old Aker Church

Damstredet

AKERSELVA

North of the city's center is the forest area called Nordmarka, and it is here that the city's largest river, Akerselva, has its source. Hydroelectric power provided by the river was instrumental in the development of many important industrial plants, but with time they created a major pollution problem. A concerted effort has been made in recent years to clean up the river – with good results. There are good stocks of trout once more in the river, and salmon has also returned.

The area alongside the river is a popular recreation area and a footpath extends from the harbor all the way up to the reservoir, Maridalsvannet, in Nordmarka. Nearby the reservoir at Kjelsås is Norsk Teknisk Museum, a national museum for technology, industry and science. Among the items exhibited here are Norway's first car, tram and airplane. It is a very popular museum, especially for children and teenagers.

THE MUSEUMS AT BYGDØY

Many of the city's most important museums are located at Bygdøy. It is possible to take a ferry there from the pier in front of Oslo City Hall during the summer months, but there are also good bus connections to the museums. Norsk Folkemuseum (Norwegian Folk Museum), a cultural heritage museum, has a total of 155 buildings from almost all regions of the country, and is one of the largest open-air museums in Europe. Here you can experience the daily life of a farming community of bygone days at your leisure.

Every part of the country is represented so that it is possible to examine the particular customs and architectural traditions of each county.

The greatest attraction at Folkemuseet is the stave Church from Gol that dates back to the year 1200 A.D. The church was originally built in Hallingdal.

Many of the old log cabins are from the Middle Ages, but the museum also includes 100-year-old buildings from Christiania, which was the city's name before it reclaimed its original name of Oslo.

Not far from Norsk Folkemuseum is the Viking Ship Museum, containing the Oseberg ship, the Gokstad ship and the Tune ship. These elegant and seaworthy ships were built between 800 and 900 A.D. Two of them are in amazingly good condition. The Oseberg ship was discovered in Slagen in Vestfold in 1904 and represents one of the riches finds from the Viking era in Norway. The Gokstad Ship contained a chamber where chieftains were entombed in beds made of ornately carved wood. They were buried along with wagons, weapons and other intricately handcrafted tools and artifacts. The ship was then buried in clay and turf. The clay was so compact that it created an airtight compartment around the ship, which prevented it from rotting.

The other museums at Bygdøy are only a short walk from here. The Fram museum houses the world famous polar ship Fram, built by the boat designer Colin Archer, and used during the three great polar expeditions: Fridtjof Nansen's voyage to the North Pole in 1893-96, Otto Sverdrup's expedition to Greenland from 1898 to 1902 and Roald Amundsen's voyage to the South Pole from 1910 to 1912, an expedition that brought Amundsen to the South Pole, but cost Scott his life. The boat is constructed with an exaggerated curve in its hull so that the ice could not take hold. Getting packed down in the ice was the most common cause of shipwreck on polar expeditions.

The Oseberg Ship is one of the world's most well-preserved Viking ships. The ship was unearthed

Norway was for many years one of the world's leading shipping nations. The anchor in front of the Norwegian Maritime Museum at Bygdøy is a symbol of this proud history.

...04, from a grave that also contained jewelry, weapons and an ornately carved wagon.

Thor Heyerdahl won international fame for his expeditions. He sailed with his crew from Safi in Marocco to Barbados on the balsa boat Ra II.

Norway has for many years been one of the world's leading shipping nations. Norsk Sjøfartsmuseum (the Norwegian Maritime Museum) has a fine collection of everything related to Norwegian shipping history. The development of everything from the first primitive boats made of hollowed out logs, to contemporary merchant ships is documented here. The museum encompasses smaller types of boats, models, photographs and artifacts and is an interesting museum for both children and adults.

The Kon-Tiki Museum houses the vessels and finds of the scientist and adventurer Thor Heyerdahl's expeditions. The main attraction of course is the Kon-Tiki raft built of nine large balsa logs, which was used on the voyage from Callo in Peru to Raroia in Polynesia in 1947, a journey of 8000 kilometers, done in 101 days. Here you will also find the papyrus boat Ra II that Heyerdahl and his crew sailed from Safi in Marokko to Barbados. Heyerdahl's voyages proved that vessels could have crossed the Atlantic Ocean in ancient times.

Bygdøy Kongsgård is the king's private farm and summer residence. The royal hunting lodge Oscarshall at Bygdøy is open to the public during the summer season. It was built by King Oscar I for entertaining purposes and not as a residence. The Danish architect Johan Henrik Nebelong's design was inspired by the gothic castles of England. The castle, and the beautiful park surrounding it, is a protected little clenodium well worth a visit. Not least because the paintings in the large hall are by Norway's leading National Romanticists, Hans Gude and Adolph Tidemand.

Bygdøy is not only known for its museums. The small peninsula is ideal for long walks, and one of the city's most popular beaches, Huk, is situated at its tip just minutes away from the city.

The Beach at Huk.

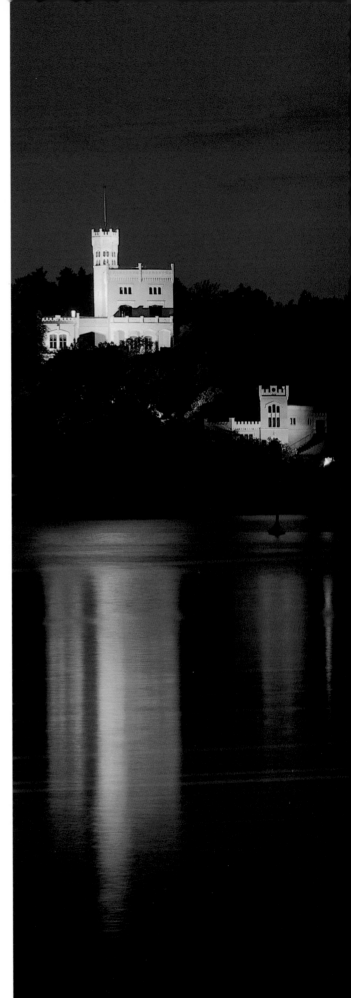

Oscarshall

NORDMARKA

Few other capitals of the world provide such fantastic possibilites for outdoor activities as Oslo. Regardless of how urban Oslo's inhabitants appear to be, on weekends they flock to the large forest that surrounds the city and provides such a wonderful setting for outdoor recreational activities.

Animal life here is abundant. It is not unusual to meet up with a moose, a fox or a hare, and there are fish in the forest lakes: trout, perch and char. There are footpaths and dirt roads everywhere for those of you who wish to go hiking or take a bicycle ride through the woods.

In winter there is a large network of ski trails for cross-country skiing.

Taking the tram to Frognerseteren can be a good place to start. You can begin your hike in the woods from the end station at the top, or stroll down to Frognerseter restaurant and enjoy a cup of hot chocolate and the restaurant's famous apple cake, before continuing downhill to the Holmenkollen Ski Jump and the Ski Museum.

A chair sled is a Norwegian phenomenon; a quick and easy way to travel on snowcovered roads.

Ullevålseter in Nordmarka is a popular destination for cross-country skiers as well as horseback riders on a sunny day.

Frognerseteren Restaurant also has one of the city's finest views. The Restaurant's apple cake with whipped cream is legendary.

Holmenkollen Park Hotel

The Ski Museum

HOLMENKOLLEN

The area surrounding Holmenkollen Ski Jump is the arena for the
annual Holmenkollen Race. The
World Championship for Ski
Jumping in 1930, The Winter
Olympics in 1952, The World
Championship for Winter Sports
in 1966 and 1982 are some of the
most important ski jumping
competitions that have taken place
here. The Tower at the top of the
slope is 60 meters high and its
highest point is 417 meters above
sea level and offers a spectacular
view of large parts of Oslo and
Nordmarka.

Legend has it that Norwegians
are "born with skis on their feet".
One mustn't take this quite literally
but let there be no mistake, skis
have been and still are an important
form of communication and source
of recreational pleasure. You can
get a good impression of the
importance of skiing for the entire
Norwegian population by visiting
the Ski Museum, located behind
the Holmenkollen Ski Jump. The
museum encompasses the history of
Norway as a nation of polar explo-
rers as well, first and foremost
represented by Fridtjof Nansen and
Roald Amundsen's South Pole
expeditions.

Bogstad

To the west of Holmenkollen is
Bogstadvannet, with its beautiful
Bogstad Estate and Bogstad Golf
Course. It is one of the city's most
popular outdoor recreation areas.

THE CITY OF FESTIVALS

The Oslo Jazz Festival, The Oslo Chamber Music Festival, The Oslo Film Festival, the Ultima Contemporary Music Festival, the Ibsen Festival and the Island Festival are some of the more important events that are arranged in Oslo. They represent some of the cultural highlights the city has to offer. Oslo has long been one of the world's leading jazz capitals, and the city's symphony orchestra, the Oslo Philharmonic Orchestra, has for many years gained a reputation for being one of the world's leading interpreters of classical music. Aside from these important events, there are numerous activities on the street level; in clubs, large and small concert halls, outdoor stages and small intimate performance locales that confirm Oslo's status as a cultural capital.

The Island Festival is arranged each year in the Oslo Medieval Park in Gamlebyen. The Festival has become a display window for upcoming Norwegian performers, and is proof that Norwegian bands are ready for success, both at home and abroad.

Following page:
Medieval Tournaments, jesters, beggars, historic plays, Medieval music and song. The Medieval Festival is a colourful, multi-national event that is fun for children and adults of all ages.

SPORTS EVENTS

The Grete Waitz Marathon, the Oslo Boat Race and Norway Cup. The internationally renowned runner Grete Waitz has a marathon named after her in Oslo. During a weekend in May each year, Norwegian women descend onto the capital to participate in the world's largest marathon for women.

In late July, early August, Oslo's appearance changes once again. This time youth from all over the world can be seen in the streets and in the city's sports arenas — it is time for the Norway Cup, the world's largest soccer tournament. 1,219 teams from 25 countries, over 25,000 soccer players, both girls and boys, from 10 to 18 years of age, participate in the event.

A more recent popular spectator sport is the Oslo Boat Race in the inner Oslo Fjord. The competition attracts world-class boat racers from all over the world, and a large public as well.

TUSENFRYD

Children and teenagers looking for action can visit the amusement park Tusenfryd, which is only a half-hour drive from downtown Oslo. The amusement park has rides and games for every age group, but the most exciting attraction is without a doubt the Thunder Coaster. This roller coaster ride is built in wood to insure the right amount of flexibility. It is steeper than the ski jump at Holmenkollen and can reach a speed of 100 kilometers per hour. It takes two minutes to drive 1 kilometer and has been chosen as Europe's best roller coaster ride. Its scary – and lots of fun!

So welcome to Oslo, the city that has something for everyone – both young and old. A city for all seasons.

Welcome to the Viking Capital!

© N.W. Damm & Søn AS
N - 0055 Oslo

Author: Helge Baardseth
Picture editor: Sissel Holt Boniface
Design: Sissel Holt Boniface
Translations: English: Francesca M. Nichols
German: Marlis Ehl
French: Claude Ceselli
Spanish: Jorunn Hiorth
Prepress: Capella Media, Norway
Printing: Nørhaven Book, 2007
4. printing

This book is published in cooperation with
VisitOslo.

visitOSLO

Captions for full-page illustrations:

PHOTOGRAPHERS:
Top = A. Top left = B. Top right = C.
Bottom = D. Bottom left = E. Bottom right = F.
Middle = G. Middle left = H. Middle right = I

Samfoto:
Bård Løken: 14, 15, 22, 23ADG, 29F, 46A/BONO
2002, 52I, 53, 62D, 75C, 78A, 80, 83E, 86.
Espen Bratlie: 16E, 36, 55E, 70B, 71D, 83H, 88,
74A /Front page C, Front page H.
Jørn Areklett Omre: 50D, 16F, 66, 67E, 70F.
Kim Hart: 4, 16, 47D, 68, 72.
Olsen/Sørensen: 33E, 55F, 65C.
Bjørn Rørslett: 8, 54D.
Jørn B. Olsen: 24.
Ole Daniel Enersen: 30B.
Ole Åsheim: 38.
Pål Hermansen: 62A.
Trygve Bølstad: 32A.
Øystein Søbye: 11.

Gunnar Strøm: 13F, 30E, 32D, 35, 42D, 42A,
43CE, 44A, 46D, 51, 52D, 55H, 56D, 79EF, 83.

Terje Rakke: 18, 27, 41F, 52B/BONO 2002, 52C,
61AG, 67AI, 70F, 75EI, 74D, Front page EF.

Knudsen, Oslo: 12, 44G, 48B/BONO 2002,
49/BONO 2002, 50A, 50A, 58, 59F, 58, 64, 76,
78D, 17F.
Knudsen/Jarlid: 26.

Megapix:
Ragnar Ness: 39.
Urpo Tarpanen: 28A.
Møyfrid Husmo: 2, 20H, Front page B.
Katarina Dufva: Front page I.
Trond Emblemsvåg: 28D.

Frits Solvang: 13E, 21, 25A, 71A.

Norgesfoto - Pål Bugge: 6/BONO 2002, 25D, 40,
45, 57.

Nancy Bundt: 31, 60, 44D, 1, Back page, End paper.

Sjøberg: Opitz: 56A. Tor Lindseth: 29E.

Helge Baardseth/BONO 2002: 37F.

Nationaltheateret/Marit-Anna Evanger: 34.

Vigelandmuseet: Siri Berrefjord /BONO 2002: 48E.

Barnekunstmuseet: 33F.

Norsk Folkemuseum/Anne-Lise Reinsfelt: 61D.

Kontiki-museet: 63D.

Munchmuseet/BONO 2002: 54C.

Tusenfryd/Ole Walter Jacobsen: 84.

Scanpix:
Erlend Aas: 25D
Jan Petter Lyran: 44A